Indiana State Christian Conference

First Annual Catalogue and Year-Book

of the Indiana State Conference of the Christian denomination, and of the

district conferences in the state of Indiana

Indiana State Christian Conference

First Annual Catalogue and Year-Book
of the Indiana State Conference of the Christian denomination, and of the district conferences in the state of Indiana

ISBN/EAN: 9783337264208

Printed in Europe, USA, Canada, Australia, Japan

Cover: Foto ©Lupo / pixelio.de

More available books at **www.hansebooks.com**

First Annual Catalogue

and

YEAR-BOOK,

of the

Ind'a State Conference

of the

Christian Denomination,

and of the

District Conferences

in the State of Indiana,

1880-81.

PRINTED AT THE CHRISTIAN AGE OFFICE, BY D. W. JONES.

FORT WAYNE, INDIANA.

Indi'a. State Christian Conference.

——:o:——

ORGANIZED AT CASSVILLE, OCTOBER 28th, 1877.
INCORPORATED AT MARION, OCTOBER 25th, 1878.

——:o:——

OFFICERS:

President,   REV. JOHN T. PHILLIPS, *Graysville.*
Vice Pres.   "   PETER WINEBRNNER, *Merriam.*
Secretary,   "   DAVID W. JONES, *Fort Wayne.*
Treasurer,   "   DAVID S. DAVENPORT, *Harrisville.*

Trustees: "   GEORGE ABBOTT, *Liberty Mills.*
          "   DAVID W. FOWLER, *Wabash City.*
          "   DAVID W. JONES, *Fort Wayne.*
          "   WATSON LUDLOW, *Veedersburg.*
          JOHN B. HANN, *Indianapolis.*
          JOHN MOSS, *Beechy Mire, Union Co.*

REV. WM. S. MANVILLE, *General Financial Agent.*

Indiana State Christian Conference.

——:o:——

THIS State Conference was fully Organized and Incorporated at a meeting held at Marion, in accordance with proper notice given in the year 1878, and by duly electing Officers, Trustees, etc.

OFFICERS:

President, J. T. PHILLIPS,
Secretary, D. W. JONES,
Treasurer, D. S. DAVENPORT.

Trustees: John Byrkitt, James Pepper, G. W. Webster, Watson Ludlow, D. W. Fowler and George Abbott.

The Trustees elected proceeded agreeably to law to cast lots, in order to decide which two of the trustees should retire at the expiration of one year, and of two years, and of three years, respectively. By virtue of said lots cast, John Byrkitt and James Pepper were to retire at the expiration of one year, and G. W. Webster and W. Ludlow at the expiration of two years, and D. W. Fowler and George Abbott at the expiration of three years.

Several meetings had been held prior to this one, but this one completed the organization. G. B. Stewart, of Wakarusa, was given an Agency, who took several hundred dollars in notes, which amount was raised mainly in Elkhart County.

SECOND ANNUAL MEETING.

The State Conference met in its Second Annual Session in Marion, Grant Co., October 21, 1879.

Officers: As above.

ADDRESS.

The opening address was delivered by Prest. T. C. Smith.

Two Trustees were elected to fill the vacancies caused by the expiration of the terms of J. Byrkitt and James Pepper. D. W. Jones was duly elected to fill the place of John Byrkitt, and J. B. Hann the place of J. Pepper.

STATE AGENT.

Elder W. S. Manville's services had been engaged for several months as State Agent.

At this session he was appointed as General Agent for the State, and so contracted with by the Trustees. Entering into a bond for the faithful performance of all the duties pertaining to the Agency.

The Committee appointed for the purpose, reported that the Conference meet in its next Annual Session in the Hagarstown Christian Church, on Thursday, after the fourth Sabbath in October, 1880. Adjourned to meet at the above named time and place.

SESSION AT HAGARSTOWN.

The Third Annual Session (called in the Christian Age the Fourth Annual Session of the Indiana State Christian Conference, which includes all the Annual State meetings; while we recon from the time the Conference became a Legal Body,) of the Indiana State Christian Conference convened in the Christian Church in Hagarstown, on Thursday, the 28th day of October, 1880, at 10 o'clock. A. M.

OFFICERS.

President,   J. T. PHILLIPS,
Vice Prest., W. A. BELL,
Secretary,   D. W. JONES,
Ass't Sec'y, C. V. STRICKLAND,
Treasurer,   D. S. DAVENPORT.

Elder E. W. Humphrey, of Yellow Springs, read a portion of Scripture, and proceeded to make some introductory remarks.

Singing by the congregation, led by Brother Strickland, of the Eel River Conference.

Prayer was offered by Elder C. W. Choate, of Covington, Ohio, and singing of the 766th Hymn by the congregation followed, after which the President declared the Conference was open for businesst

PROGRAMME.

1. Reception of Delegates,
2. Misssion Board Report,
3. Receiving Letters,
4. Appointing Committees,
5. Election of Officers,
6. Report of Officers,
7. Unfinished Business,
8. Miscellaneous Business.

ROLL OF CONFERENCES WITH DELEGATES.

1.   CENTRAL CONFERENCE.
P. J. Baker, J. W. Carney, A. S. Downey and B. Carmichael.

2.   EASTERN CONFERENCE.

R. M. Hayworth. J. C. Kershner, E. Burch, W. Chennowith. T. A. Burns and J. Newhouse.

3.   EEL RIVER CONFERENCE.

C. V. Strickland. W. D. Samuels, S. McNeely and Peter Winebrenner.

4.   GRANT COUNTY CONFERENCE.

No delegates.

5.   SOUTHERN INDIANA CONFERENCE.

President T. C. Smith.

6.   NORTH-WESTERN CONFERENCE.

W. Y. Winegardner, K. E. West and Dr. M. N. Wooley.

7.   U. M. RESERVE CONFERENCE.

J. R. Kobb, P. L. Ryker, S. Rains and J. L. Puckett.

8.   WESTERN INDIANA CONFERENCE.

W. T. Warbinton, J. T. Phillips, W. Ludlow. A. L. Carney and L. W. Bannon.

VISITING BRETHREN.

Elders A. W. Coan, C. W. Garroutte, E. W. Humphries and Rev. Choate, Ohio; G. B. Fuller, Michigan; Dr. Keith, Ohio; also Elder Moore and wife, Rev. J. M. Mann, W. C. Bowen and others.

HAGARSTOWN CHURCH.

Upon this Church there was found to rest a debt of about $1,500, which the State Conference assumed. The Trustees obligating to deed the church over to the State Conference.

Elder D. W. Fowler was appointed a Special Agent to canvass the State for funds to pay off the debt; and was put under bonds, for the faithful performance of the same.

GENERAL AGENT.

Elder Manville was continued General Agent with full powers to continue the canvass of the State.

During the last year's canvass the Agent reports in notes and cash some $11,000. There is now in the Treasury, in notes, some over $15,000. Thus it will be seen that our Agent has not been idle, and that our people have done nobly. The interest in this State work is on the rise, and may it continue until we have ample funds, the interest of which may be sufficient to fully sustain the Christian cause in all parts of our beloved Zion.

ADDRESS.

The Opening Address was delivered by Elder Peter Winebrenner, which address was voted a place in this Catalogue.

Committee on Catalogue: D. W. Jones, J. T. Phillips and P. Winebrenner. After which Peter Winebrenner was appointed Chairman, and ordered to go on with the publication of the same at the very earliest convenience, by the middle of January, if possible.

The Christian Age and Union Christian College both received due attention, and were fully discussed. Conference sustaining the Trustees in their contract with the editor of the Christian Age.

The election of two Trustees to fill the places of Watson Ludlow and G. W. Webster, whose terms expired at this Conference.

Watson Ludlow and John Moss were duly elected said Trustees for the term of three years.

The Board of Trustees now stands:

WATSON LUDLOW, *Veedersburg,* three years.
JOHN MOSS, *Union County,* three years.
D. W. JONES. *Fort Wayne,* two years.
J. B. HANN. *Indianapolis,* two years.
D. W. FOWLER. *Wabash City,* one year.
GEORGE ABBOTT, *Liberty Mills,* one year.

OFFICERS ELECT.

President, J. T. PHILLIPS. *Graysville, Indiana.*
Vice Prest.. P. WINEBRENNER, *Merriam,* "
Secretary, D. W. JONES. *Fort Wayne,* "
Treasurer, D. S. DAVENPORT, *Harrisville,* "
General Agt., W. S. MANVILLE, *Valparaiso,* "
Special Agt., D. W. FOWLER. *Wabash City,* "

Conference Adjourned to meet again at Hagarstown, in October, 1881.

Benediction by Elder George Abbott.

J. T. PHILLIPS. *President.*

D. W. JONES, *Secretary.*

CONSTITUTION

OF THE

Indiana State Conference,

------:0:------

WHEREAS, The Christians of the State of Indiana have felt, long and deeply, the want of co-operation among ministers, churches, and conferences in general enterprises, and of harmony and uniformity in local affairs: therefore, for the " better work of the ministry, the perfecting of the saints, the edifying of the body of Christ," we, the delegates from the several local conferences of the State of Indiana, in conference assembled at Cassville, Howard County, October 24 and 25, 1877, do adopt the following

CONSTITUTION:

ARTICLE I.—*Name.*—This body shall be known as the Indiana State Christian Conference.

ARTICLE II.—*Organization.*—The Indiana State Christian Conference shall be composed of delegates appointed by the several conferences of the State as follows:

1. Each Conference of the State shall be entitled to one Delegate as a body; and to one additional for each ten churches in number, composing such Conference.

2. These delegates shall be properly accredited in writing to the Secretary of the State Conference by the Secretary or Clerk of Conference sending them.

ARTICLE III.—*Officers.*—The Officers of this Conference shall be a President, Vice-President, Secretary, and Treasurer, whose duties shall be the same as in other similar bodies.

1. They shall be elected by ballot at each annual session, and shall serve for the term of one year, but shall not enter upon the duties of their respective offices until the beginning of the annual session next following their election.

ARTICLE IV.—*Board of Trustees.*—The Board of Trustees shall consist of six members, who shall be elected by ballot and apportioned among the several Conferences of the State as fairly as may be done, who shall serve for the term of three years.

1. Four, including the President, shall constitute a quorum for the transaction of business.

2. The first Board shall be organized as is provided by Statue, by determining by lot the time they shall serve, one third for one year, one-third for two years, and one-third for three years.

3. The President and Secretary of the State Conference shall be *ex-officio* President and Secretary of the Board of Trustees.

4. The Board of Trustees shall elect the Treasurer, not from their own number, and shall exercise such power, and perform such duties as may be delegated and referred to it by the general body.

ARTICLE V.—*Meetings.*—The regular meetings of this Conference shall assemble annually at 2 P. M., Tuesday before the last Sunday in October, at such place as may be agreed upon by the Conference.

1. Special meetings may be called by the President and Secretry, or by any five Trustees.

ARTICLE VI.—*Amendment.*—This Constitution may be changed at any regular session of this body by giving notice of the same in our publications, naming the parts to be amended at least three months before the session at which the motion is to be made.

Annual Conference Address,

---:o:---

TEXT—*Gal.* 2: 6; and *Acts* 15.

The word Conference means: The examination of things in the way of comparison. To consult together—To confer.

We are here for the purpose of confering together for the furtherance of our beloved Christianity. May we be somewhat to each other in Conference, and may the Spirit of the Divine Master guide us into all truth, and be manifested in all our deliberations. We will notice:

I. The rise of our State Christian Conference:

This is of but recent date: a preliminary meeting was held at Marion, July 28th, 1877.

The First Annual Session was held at Cassville, October 28th, 1877. Three annual Sessions are past: we are now in our fourth one.

We have had, however, less than two years work, done by a regular State Agent, for the purpose of raising means for the Sinking Fund. Some notes, however, were taken by other agents, before the Conference fully endorsed the Sinking Fund system. We are yet in our infancy, but we have been profited somewhat, by the good example of our Seignionr, the Ohio State Christian Association, which is in a flourishing condition. We have succeeded in putting into the Treasury a respectable sum of money. We think we are justifiable in making this statement, when we take into consideration, that this is a new thing to the people in our State. In fact, some of them are surprised to think that we should undertake such a magnificent work as this—it is wondrous in their eyes.

Some time is, however, required to educate the people up to the proper standard of giving of their means, in sums sufficiently large, to carry forward to completion such a work as the State Christian Conference has in contemplation.

II. We will next notice the Conferences which compose this State Conference. These are eight in number. We have not been enabled as yet to get a full statistical account of these Conferences ; hence we can only give them in part. We will give their names severally, in the order in which they are spread upon the minutes of the last Annual Session of Conference.

1. The Central Christian Conference.
2. " Eastern Indiana Conference.
3. " Eel River Conference.
4. " Grant County Conference.
5. " Southern Indiana Conference.
6. " North-Western Conference.
7. " Union Miami Reserve Conference.
8. " Western Indiana Conference.

The Western Indiana Conference has celebrated its 50th Anniversary. Hence was organized fifty years ago ; and I am happy to say, that its last session is said to have been one of even unusual interest,—one of the very best.

The Eel River Conference has just passed its Thirty-Seventh Anniversary. This Conference was organized August 26, 1844, with three ordained, and six licensed ministers : eight churches ; aggregated membership, 258. It numbers at present : ministers 31 : churches 31 : total membership over 2,200.

Father correct statistics I cannot give, but hope that we will get them during this Conference Session. I presume that we have a membership within the State of Indiana of over 20,000, and this membership controls no small amount of wealth : from which amount there should be enough donated to endow the State Conference for all intents and purposes, to carry forward its great mission work.

Our predecessors have done a noble work for us. Theirs was hard toil and labour. They traveled sometimes on foot, and some of them bare-footed at that ; sometimes on horse-back or in a wagon, upon the Indian trail, or a winding wagon road, running around timber falls, called dead falls : and swamps, through marshes : in short any way and any how, so that they might be enabled to reach their appointments.

Then the Brethren would bring out their families, either on foot, horse-back, or in wagons, with, sometimes, an ox team ; or occasionally, a family ox would bear upon its back its load of human beings to the house of the Lord, which was a log cabin : and usually the humble dwelling of some devoted Christian family, composed frequently of one room. This answered for kitchen, parlor, bed room and church ; seated with stools, flat rails, and the family beds. Later cabin school houses were erected. If the services were in the evening, there could be seen in the different directions along the winding paths, the approach of the hickory-bark torch-light, which lit up the winding paths of devoted christians and their neighbors, all marching to the house of worship, where they attentively listened to the Word of Life, as expounded to them by the Man of God, an humble self-sacrificing Minister of Jesus Christ. Those efforts were greatly blessed to the conversion of many precious souls.

Churches were organized, and these in due time were formed into Conferences, all over our then wilderness country, but now garden State. In those early times, the cause of our well beloved Master, Christ Jesus, was moved forward with but little financial aid. Our Fathers labored in the Ministry, with scarcely any, and sometimes, with no salary at all. But time moved on; grain fields took the place of the mighty forests; the Indian and the wild beast measureably disappeared. School houses were erected, then colleges. And here we are to-day, over fifty years in the advance. The forest has melted away before the hand of civilization, the result of christian advancement.

Now all over our State are beautiful, rich and productive farms. The log cabin is superceded by magnificent dwellings. The wild plum and crab-apple thickets, by orchards, bearing all the varieties of delicious fruits. Then think of our Villages, Towns and Cities, with their manufacturing facilties; our mercantile wealth, etc.

Also think of our conveniences for travel: our wagon roads abundant, piked and graveled. All the large streams well bridged; prancing horses; flashy harness; cushion-seated carriages. Oh! with what ease we now travel! What a contrast to the Indian trail, winding road, rough, jostling wagon, compared with our soft cushioned seats, and these upon pliable springs. Are we now content? or are we grumbling on yet, and sighing for the times of yore; and these we call private conveyances.

Then what of public conveyances? Our railroads—their speed, so that distance is measured by time, and not by miles. Now a few hundred miles are passed as quickly as a few miles were in ancient times. Think of the comfort also, of riding in palace coaches. The winds may blow, the rain may fall, storms rage, but here we are as comfortable as if we were at home in the old arm chair.

Then, consider also, the no small number of Church edifices we have all over the State. Also the common schools, the high schools, and our beloved Union Christian College, with our CHRISTIAN AGE, books, etc.; great population and a vast amount of wealth. With all this before us, we are made to exclaim; That the look-out for us, is certainly very cheering, and promises great events. And we flatter ourselves that by doing our part well, and making use, properly, of the means within our reach, that the most cheering results, which the most sanguine might anticipate, will be the outcoming, growing fruits of the work of this Conference. Brethren, be encouraged and go on in your work of honoring God in the salvation of precious souls.

III. For the furtherance of Christ's cause, and the growth of Christianity, we advise the appointing of Committees as follows:

1. On the evil of Drunkenness and its Remedy.

We ask this Committee, aside from the Committee, on Temperance. The crying evil of drunkenness being too great, to be connected with other branches of intemperance, such as tobacco, etc.

2. Committee on Temperance, aside from the use of ardent spirits.

3. On Sunday Schools.

4. On CHRISTIAN AGE. Its finance, and how to increase its circulation.

5. On Publications—the whole work.

6. On Union Christian College, in all its several departments, with its claims on the Christian Denomination, and the Denomition on the College.

We do not believe that a Committe on Education, could consider every department and thing, connected with the Union Christian College. Hence we ask for a Committee to give all its energies to Union Christian College alone.

7. On Education.

8. On Auditing Accounts.

9. On Finance.

10. On Moral Reform.

11. Advice to the Ministry, and the Relation which they sustain to the Church.

12. On Advice to the Laity, and the Relationship which they sustain to the Ministry.

13. On Mission Work. To begin without delay.

14. On Closing Exercises.

Thus far we have confined our remarks to the State of Indiana alone. We now come to our general work; for we being a part of the whole, have an interest at large, in common, with our Brethren, in the working and interests of the people called Christians.

IV. Our Cause at Large.

1. Our Rise. With this we go much farther back than with our own State. Instead of being a little over fifty years ago, it is nearly a century ago. The Christians started up anew, East, West, North and South, nearly simultaneously. This uniform up-rising we claim to be of Divine origin.

2. Our Progress. This has been gradual, but constant and steady onward. The little cloud or mound, at first, has become a great mountain. The Denomination is now exerting a wholesome influence over the several States and Canada. And its principles are felt, and acknowledged pretty extensively among the different Denominations throughout Christendom. And they (the Denominations) are more of a Bible people, and have a more extended fellowship for each other, and are doing more good in the world than before our rise, from the fact of the organization of the Christian Connection, as the principle of uniting with all Chris-

tians upon the Bible is a basis, which cannot consistently be opposed.

3. Our Work is to be continued. Yes, for our Work is not yet done.

While much has been done under unfavorable circumstances, when we were weak and poor, now that we have attained to greater wealth and strength, certainly much more can now be done. Under less favorable circumstances we have organized Churches, formed these into Conferences; and these district Conference into State Conferences; and those again into one grand Quadrennial Conference of the whole. We have aided and sent out missionaries, to labor in the fields. Have erected and partially endowed colleges. Have established periodicals, published books, sending out our literature pretty extensively.

Probably we have not done this work as thoroughly as we should have done it. But certainly much has been done. Let us go on to a higher state of perfection. We may do this by completing the well-begun work; and to do this well, we must place our Schools, Publications, and Missionary Work beyond the reach of want. And then you may be well assured that general prosperity will attend each and every department of our great work. The dissemination of truth, and the upbuilding of the Master's cause.

Just so long as sin abounds, and some are unconverted, infidelity existing, and the union of God's people upon the Bible not completed, so long the mission of the Christians will continue, legitimately, and in full force.

4. How to Work. We should work in harmony with each other.

By this we do not mean that we should not contend with each other on our differences. For we are to contend earnestly for the sainted Faith. But we are to do this in the spirit of Christ Jesus, and not in a spirit of strife, therby causing unnecessary division, remembering that we can understand the words spoken by the Son of God just as well as any other book, which was at first written in another tongue, and in ancient times.

Truly, the sayings of Jesus are to be spiritually discerned. Then having the Spirit of Christ we may understand his word. We are not to give up what we believe to be Bible doctrine, unless our best judgement is convinced by Bible evidence, that we were mistaken in our views of the subject under consideration; and being convinced of our error, we should at once frankly acknowledge our mistake—give it up, and just as earnestly, and if possible more earnestly—contend for what we are now satisfied is the doctrine taught by the Son of God, remembering that His word will judge us in the last day.

And we are all, no doubt, fully convinced, that as a denomination, we should fully endow all of our Schools, and lift our Publishing House out of the mire of debt. And as a State, we should lead out in all the interests of Union Christian College; that we should also sustain. and put the Christian Age beyond all embarrassment.

Also to so increase the State Conference sinking fund that it may be in all time to come enabled to meet all demands; heeding all calls for aid, in building up our beautiful Zion throughout the State. until righteousness shall cover it, as the waters cover the great deep. And not only our State. but the whole World, until earth shall keep jubilee, and the will of God be done. on earth as it it is done in Heaven. May God grant it, and that right spedily. AMEN.

Union Christian College.

:0:

A BRIEF NOTICE, HISTORY, LOCATION, BUILDING, REGULATIONS, CALENDAR FOR 1880 AND 1881, BOARD OF TRUSTEES, EXECUTIVE COMMITTEE, FACULTY, ALUMNI, ETC.

:0:

LOCATION.

Union Christian College is located at Merom, Sullivan County, Indiana. The most convenient station is Sullivan, on the Evansville & Terre Haute Railroad, twenty-six miles south of Terre Haute, and thirty-two north of Vincennes. A hack runs daily between Merom and Sullivan, a distance of ten miles.

A narrow guage railroad is in course of construction from Bedford, Indiana, to Quincy, Illinois, passing through Sullivan, Merom, and Robinson, Illinois. It is hoped that it will be in operation by July 1, 1880.

Merom, the former county-seat, is situated in the western part of the county, on the Wabash River. It is unsurpassed in the Mississippi Valley for the romance and attractiveness of its situation, being located on a high and precipitous bluff overlooking the waters of the Wabash, the prairies of Indiana above and below, and those of Illinois beyond. Its population is about six hundred. The morals, order and quiet of the place are not surpassed and rarely equalled. Grog-shops and gambling-saloons are unknown in the town, and allurements to dissipation and objects that distract the mind from study are few.

BUILDING.

The College edifice is a magnificent structure of brick, one hundred and nine feet long, sixty-five broad, sixty-three feet to top of front wing walls, eighty-eight feet to floor of cupola, one hundred and twenty-eight feet to top of central spire. It is four stories high; comprises twenty-six commodious apartments; and, from the cupola, the eye sweeps an area of more than one thousand square miles.

REGULATIONS.

The rules of the institution are few. They extend to those subjects only which are essential to order, morals, and successful study, such as a faithful and industrious student would impose upon himself.

CALENDAR.

——:o:——

1880.

June 8.—Annual Meeting of Stockholders and Trustees.
June 9.—Spring Term Closes—Commencement Day.
September 8.—Fall Term Commences.
December 1.—Fall Term Closes.
December 8.—Winter Term Commences.

1881.

March 9.—Winter Term Closes.
March 16.—Spring Term Commences.
June 7.—Annual Meeting of Stockholders and Trustees.
June 8.—Spring Term Closes—Commencement Day.
September 7.—Fall Term Commences.
November 30.—Fall Term Closes.
December 7.—Winter Term Commences.
(Regular examination of classes begins on last Monday morning of each term.)

——:o:——

BOARD OF TRUSTEES.

REV. T. C. SMITH, A. M., Pres't;   PROF. B. F. McHENRY, Sec'y.

	Conference Represented.	*Time Expires.*
JOHN L. BLANCHARD, ESQ.	Spoon River, Illinois.	
REV. E. W. HUMPHREY	Southern, Ohio	1880
JOHN VAN MATER, ESQ.	Miami, Ohio	1880
REV. PETER WINEBRENNER	Eel River, Indiana	1880
REV. D. M. SHOEMAKER, A. M.	Mazon River, Illinois	1880
F. P. McCLAIN, ESQ.	Central, Illinois	1881
R. C. WILKINSON, ESQ.	Southern, Indiana	1881
HON. GEORGE I. REED, A. M.	Tippecanoe, Indiana	1881
REV. JOHN T. PHILLIPS	Western, Indiana	1881
REV. E. A. DE VORE, A. M.	Western, Indiana	1881
REV. L. W. BANNON	Western, Indiana	1881
REV. A. R. HEATH	Western, Indiana	1882
REV. WM. T. WARBINTON	Eastern, Indiana	1882
IRA DENNEY, ESQ.	Eastern, Indiana	1882
THOMAS STANLEY, ESQ.	Miami Reserve, Indiana	1882
PROF. W. A. BELL, A. M.	Southern Wabash, Illinois	1882

——:o:——

EXECUTIVE COMMITTEE.

REV. T. C. SMITH, A. M., President.
REV. A. R. HEATH,   THOMAS STANLEY, ESQ.
REV. J. T. PHILLIPS,   F. P. McCLAIN, ESQ.
PROF. B. F. McHENRY,   THOMAS STANLEY,
     Secretary.   Treasurer,

FACULTY.

——:o:——

Rev. THOMAS C. SMITH, A. M., President,
Professor of Mental and Moral Philosophy, Logic, and Political Economy.

*J. HOWARD FORD, A. M.,
Professor of Greek and English Literature.

DAVID J. EVANS, A. M.,
Professor of Latin.

B. F. McHENRY, A. M.,
Professor of Mathematics.

Rev. JOSEPH J. SUMMERBELL, A. M.,
Non-resident Professor of Biblical Instruction.

†......................   ....
Professor of Natural Science.

†...........   ....
Professor of Modern Languages.

MISS S. E. HATTEN, A. B.,
Teacher of Greek.

BENJAMIN C. DAVIS,
Principle of Academic Department, and Professor of Elocution.

MRS. EMMA DAVIS,
Teacher of Instrumental Music.

MRS. MARIA H. McHENRY,
Teacher of Drawing and Painting.

W. P. KNODE,
Teacher of Algebra.

JOHN A. FINLEY,
Teacher of Arithmetic.

*(Absent on leave. Miss Hatten has performed the duties of this chair during the year, very acceptably.)

——————————— — ————— -

†The duties of these chairs are, for the present, performed by other members of the Faculty.

ALUMNI.

————:o:————

(S) Denotes Scientific Department.

1864.

J. J. SUMMERBELL, Minister and Non-resident Professor of Biblical Instruction U. C. C., Milford, New Jersey.

1866.

M. SELMA INGERSOLL, Principle of Ward School, Indianapolis, Ind.
G. I. REED, Editor *Republican*, Peru, Indiana.
T. C. SMITH, President U. C. College, Merom, Indiana.

1871.

D. M. SHOEMAKER, Minister, Cynthiana, Indiana.

1872.

W. H. HUMPHREY, Physician, Terre Haute, Indiana.
HOMER HICKS, (S), Professor of Mathematics, Male Seminary, Tahlequah, I. T
W. T. STILWELL, County School Superintendent, Ft. Branch, Ind.

1873.

JAMES C. DEVORE, Farmer, Higginsport, Ohio.
SARAH E. McKINNEY, Teacher, Merom, Indiana.
DRUE P. WATSON (S), Watseka, Illinois.

1874.

JOSEPHINE FORD.

1875.

HENRIETTA MASSEY (S), Teacher, Merom, Indiana.
A. M. WARD (S), Assistant Superintendent, Plymouth, Indiana.
L. F. WATSON (S), Editor *Republican*, Watseka, Illinois.
M. S. WILKINSON (S), Superintendent, Bowling Green, Indiana.

1876.

JOHN W. DAVIDSON (S), Teacher, Evansville, Indiana.
E. A. DEVORE, Minister, Ripley, Ohio.
G. R. HAMMOND, Professor, Starkey Seminary, Eddytown, N. Y.
D. T. MORGAN (S), Lawyer, Terre Haute, Indiana.
S. J. PARDEE (S), Superintendent, Wilson, New York.
M. P. WARD, Temperance Lecturer, Merom, Indiana.
JOHN WHITAKER (S), Minister, Offerle, Kansas.

1877.

FLORENCE A. M. HARVEY (S), Student, Oberlin, Ohio.
ORIETTA HEATH MORGAN (S), Merom, Indiana.
A. A. HOLMES (S), Teacher, Sullivan, Indiana.

1878.

SARAH ELIZABETH HATTEN, Teacher, U. C. C., Merom, Indiana.
REV. JOEL MYERS, Principal Weaubleau Institute, Weaubleau, Mo.
G. W. FINLEY (S), Physician, Harmony, Indiana.
EVAN W. HEATH (S), Merchant, Merom, Indiana.

1879.

JOHN SUMMERBELL BOORD (S), Teacher, Rocky Ford, Colorado.
LARUE GORDON (S), Principal, Prairie Creek, Indiana.
GEO. W. WRIGHT (S), Teacher, Flat Rock, Illinois.

Union Miami Reserve Conference.

————:o:————

Organized in the year 1852, and was at first called the Little Wild Cat Christian Conference, with officers as follows:

President, T. SCOTT,
Secretary, J. B. FRANCAISE.

First Ministers.—H. L. Puckett, A. Cole, George Bozell, S. Poff and others.

The name was changed in 1856 to Union Miami Reserve Christian Conference, which name it yet retains.

PRESENT OFFICERS:

President, JAMES RECOBS, *Tipton, Indiana*.
Secretary, J. R. KOBB, *Center, Indiana*.

NUMBER OF MINISTERS:

Ordained..............................32
Unordained...........................5
Number of Churches..............32
    "   Added this Year........434
    Total Membership...........2,079

Aggregate Amount of Pastor's Salary............................$ 1,074
Paid for Building purposes.. 1,175
Subscribed to State Mission Fund................................ 3,300
Paid State Conference... 5
Value of Church Property... 13,100
    Total Amount Raised and Paid Out...................... 2,164

SUNDAY SCHOOLS.

Number of Sunday Schools.................11
Number of Sunday School Scholars......808
Money Raised for Sunday School.............................$165

MISCELLANEOUS.

Number of Meeting Houses.................19

Delegates to the State Conference held in Hagarstown, Indiana: J. L. Pucket, S. Raines, P. L. Ryker, J. R. Kobb, and J. Fry.

The names of Churches with Secretaries and their address, Sunday School Superintendents and address, are not given. We have the name of twenty-four ministers which we record.

LIST OF MINISTERS WITH THEIR ADDRESS.

1　Laymon, John Michigantown.
2　Smith, Thomas Mier, Grant County.
3　Goldsbury, Isaac Galveston.
4　Teeter, M. L. Goldsmith.
5　Sorter, Jacob Kokomo.
6　Puckett, John L. Cassville.
6　Williams, A. C. Mechanicsburg.
8　Bozell, George Shieldsville.
9　Irby, Columbus Sharpsville.
10　Parker, William G. Summitville.
11　Hubbard, George Majenica.
12　Dipboye, Jonathan Frankton.
13　Heflin, William Rock Creek.
14　Kobb, John R. Center.
15　Harold, W. L. Russiaville.
16　Suit, John S. Alto.
17　Ryker, P. L. Goldsmith.
18　Comer, Joseph Center.
19　Comer, James Tipton.
20　Hercules, L. W. Center.
21　McClurg, M. Rock Creek.
22　Salee, N. Burlington.
23　Van Ness, F. Tipton.
24　Grovier, L. L. Frankfort.

These are all the names I find reported, yet the whole number is given at 37.

Southern Indiana Conference.

————:o:————

This Conference was organized in the year 1864, by Elders Austin Hutson, John Boren, and others. The Officers were:

President, A. H. BOREN,
Secretary, J. B. CALVERT,
Treasurer, A. B. WILKINS.

NUMBERS AT PRESENT,

Ministers Ordained...............3
     "   Unordained...........2
Number of Churches..............5

FINANCE.

Aggregate Pastor's Salary...............................$1,000
Paid Publishing House.................................... 100
Value of all Church Property............................ 5,000

MISCELLANEOUS.

Number of Meeting Houses..................3
Total Membership...........................548

Conference was incorporated in 1864.

The following persons are Secretaries of Churches, viz:

T. J. REDMAN, *Cynthiana.*
SIMON GRIM, *Evansville.*
A. B. WILKINS, *Cynthiana.*
L. J. WASSON, *Owensville.*

COUNTIES OCCUPIED.

Posey, Gibson, and Vanderburg.

Delegate to the State Conference, held at Hagartown:

T. C. SMITH, *President of Union Christian College.*

OFFICERS OF CONFERENCE.

President, A. H. BOREN, *Cynthiana.*
Secretary, J. C. CALVERT,   "
Treasurer, A. B. WILKINSON,   "

LIST OF MINISTERS AND THEIR ADDRESS.

Ordained.

1 Smith, T. C. Merom.
2 Shoemaker, D. M. Cynthiana.
3 Wright, William R. Princeton.

Unordained.

4 Beach, William Evansville.
5 Walters, William W. Bridgeport.

LIST OF CHURCHES WITH LOCATION.

1 New Liberty, Gibson County.
2 Union Christian, Vanderburg County.
3 Bethsaida, Posey County.
4 Antioch, Gibson County.
5 Pleasant View, Posey County.

Western Indiana Conference.

————:0:————

This Conference was at first organized on Saturday before the second Sunday in June, 1831, on Graham Creek, some four miles southeast of Covington. Fountain County, Indiana, by Elder Solomon McKinney. Watson Clarke, Daniel Osborn, John Hibbs, Michael Black, and James McKinney, were ordained at this meeting. The Conference was organized under the name of the Cole Creek Christian Conference. The first record shows Deacon Ira Smith, of LaFayette, *President*. Name of Secretary not given.

About the year 1840, the Tippecanoe Conference was organized, out of the northern part of this Conference; and subsequently all west of the Wabash River was organized into the Central Illinois Christian Conference. About 1844 or 45. the name was changed to that of Western Indiana Christian Conference, which name has been retained up to the present date—1880.

INCORPORATION.

The Conference was incorporated on the twentieth day of January 1874.

MINISTERS.

We have on record the names of 121 Elders; 33 deceased while members; 38 dismissed by letter; 21 removed without letter, and 5 were dismissed—The rest remain with us up to the present.

OFFICERS OF CONFERENCE.

President. J. T. PHILLIPS, *Graysville, Indiana.*
Secretary, R. M. THOMAS. *Pleasant Hill,*   "
Treasurer, W. H. GILBERT, *Staunton,*   "

MINISTERS AND MEMBERS.

1	Number of	Ordained Ministers..................	26
2	"	Unordained Ministers..................	18
3	"	Churches......	33
4	"	Male Members............................	905
5	"	Female Members.........................	1,202
6	"	Added this Year.......................	893
		Aggregate membership.................	3,060

SUNDAY SCHOOLS.

1	Number of Sunday Schools Supported........................	10
2	" Scholars.......................................	647
3	" Officers and Teachers, unknown................	
4	" Sunday School Heralds taken....................	210
5	" Other Sunday School Papers taken............	160
	Monies Raised..	$102 63

FINANCES.

Aggregate Amount of Pastor's Salary........................			$ 2,526 50
" " Paid for other Preaching..............			221 10
" " " Building Purposes...........			4,781 00
" " Paid Publishing House at Dayton...			51 00
" " " State Misson Fund.................			515 55
State Conference Fund..			8 11
Total Amount of Money Raised and Paid Out..............			3,121 25
Value of Church Property......................................			13,350 50
Church Houses, about...			25

DELEGATES TO THE STATE CONFERENCE,

Held in Hagarstown, Indiana, October, 1880: Elders Joel Thomas, W. T. Warbinton, A. L. Carney, W. Ludlow, and J. T. Phillips.

NAMES OF ORDAINED MINISTERS AND ADDRESS.

Bannon, L. W. Russell's Mill.
Carney, A. L. Boston Store.
Phillips, J. T. Graysville.
Heath, A. R. Merom.
Akeres, A. J. Pimento.
Simmonds, E. D. Steam Corners.
Hutts, L. W. Steam Corners.
Brown, J. M. Staunton.
Early, William M. Staunton.
Jones, Eliza. Terre Haute.
Wilkins, Z. M. Veedersburg.
Ludlow, Watson Veedersburg.
Parr, Jesse A. Lebanon.
Coombs, W. M. Jamestown.
Burman, J. T. Jamestown.
Martin. Jonathan Mace.
Pearce, Z. A. Hutsonville.
Warbinton. W. T. Hagarstown.
Sowers, E. P. Harveysburg.
McCoy, Linsey Waynetown.
Quillen. Thomas Crawfordsville.
Yokum. J. B. Brazil.
Quick. Edwin Crawfordsville.
Allen. T. J. Kirtland.
Philp. O. F. Watseka, Illinois.
Thomas. Joel Arcanum, Ohio.

UNORDAINED MINISTERS.

Paget, J. W. Hooserville.
Coombs, W. N. Jamestown.
Gillispie, T. C. Brazil.
Quick, Nathan Crawfordsville.
Patrick, F. M. Wallace.
Early, William Conterpoint.
Nickel, J. S. Wallace.
Compton, Squire Brazil.
Valkenburg, S. Newtown.
Beman, J. T. Jamestown.
Harper, William Waynetown.
Taylor, Thomas Crawfordsville.
Perrine, B. F.
Carr, Mrs. E. Crawfordsville.
Dooley, Mrs. M. Ludlow, Illinois.
Evans, D. J. Zanesville, Ohio.

CHURCHES:

Churches.	Secretary.	Address.
Pleasant Hill	Thomas, J. D.	Pleasant Hill, Indiana
Osborn Prairie	Timmons, Z. O.	Stonebluff, "
Merom	Evans, D. J.	Zanesville, Ohio
New Salem	Reese, J.	Thorntown, Indiana
Center School House	Daisy, D. W.	Boston Store, "
Pleasant Grove,	Ewbanks, L. C.	Russel's Mill, "
Bethany		
Bethel	Card, Bruce	Waveland, Indiana
Antioch,	Steward, Henry	Frankfort, "
Shilo	Whittington, J.	Jamestown, "
Otter Creek Union	Hoffman, E.	Brazil, "
Staunton	Modisette, Wm.	Staunton, "
U. C. Church Clay Co.	Meke, J.	Poland, "
Union Cemetry	Kiff, B. M.	Newtown, "
Darlington	Mote, Jeremiah	Darlington, "
Pleasant View	Bowen, E.	Lebanon, "
Jefferson	Anderson, J.	Jefferson, "
Harmony	Bowen, H. G.	Hillsboro, "
Mount Olive,	Peters, G. W.	Pimento, "
Center Grove	Caldwell, B. M.	Darlington, "
Liberty,	Quick, N.	Crawfordsville, "
Cold Spring	Maxwell, J. C.	Veedersburg, "
New Union	Vangandy, S. P.	Crawfordsville, "
Croy's Creek,	Johnson, R. M.	Harmony, "
Brown's Wonder,	Kern, A. C.	Lebanon, "
Mount Pleasant	Johnson, J. M.	Crawfordsville, "
Dry Run	Murray, J. T.	Pleasant Hill, "
Big Spring	Watson, R. H.	Graysville, "
Brown's School House		
Spring Hill	Brown, J. M.	Steam Corners, Indiana
Christian Chapel,	Stowars, J.	Kirk's Cross Roads, "

Lamont's Prairie..........Pearce, Z. A..................Palestine, Illinois
U. C. Church,..............Gillispy, T. C................Poland, Indiana
Union Chapel..............Ward, S..........................Mace,   "
Center Grove..............Osburn, S. G.........Harveysburg,   "
Mount Vernon..
West Union..
Brush Creek...
Westfield...
Jacksonville...
Union, Owen Co..

This gives us a total of forty-one Churches; eight, however, has not reported; leaving us thirty-three Churches which have reported. How much a full report of those eight Churches would swell the aggregate membership, we have no means at hand of knowing. To the correctness of the above report the Conference Secretary, R. M. Thomas, has certified, and affixed thereunto the seal of said Conference, from which I have taken this copy.

Eel River Conference.

————:o:————

The Eel River Christian Conference was organized on Eel River, Kosciousko County, August 26th, 1844.

Prayer was offered by Elder James Atchison. Elder A. Baldwin was chosen Chairman, and Brother W. B. Wade Secretary. Elder Snethen delivered the opening address.

By resolution, the Conference was called the Eel River Christian Conference, which name it has ever through its history of thirty-seven years, retained.

MEMBERS OF THE ORGANIZATION.

Amos Baldwin, John Plummer, and Samuel Pfoff.

LICENTIATES.

Willis Thompson, Levi Abbott, David Monroe, John Pfoff, Benjamin Montgommery, Henderson Johnson, W. Deal, and W. Shelly. Eight Licentiates. Total Ministers 11.

CHURCHES AND THEIR MEMBERSHIP.

1	Deal's Creek	26
2	Miami Reserve	26
3	Wabash	23
4	Eel River	65
5	Washington	15
6	Wolf Lake	12
7	Waterford	44
8	Leesburg	50
9	Chippeway Notch	23
	Churches	9

Total Membership................284

Ordained Ministers.............. 3
Licensed   " 11

These are the charter members of Eel River Conference over thirty-seven years ago.

Time, place, and names of the officers of each session of Conference since its organization.
Second year, 1845.

> *President,* ELIAS BAKER,
> *Secretary,* W. B. WADE,
> *Address,*   By SNOW RITCHISON, of Ohio.

Members received during Conference session:—Elders Joseph Roberds and James Atchison.

LICENTIATES.

David Bowser, Squire Wood, and W. S. Baker.

CHURCHES RECEIVED.

Pleasant Grove, Members........................20
Tremble Creek,   "   6
Pleasant Hill,   "   8

THIRD SESSION.

Held near Waterford, Elkhart County, August 13th, 1846.
Address by Elder J. Roberds.

MEMBERS RECEIVED.

Ministers: Elders Sacket and McCollum.   Licentiate, E. Thacker.

> *President,* JOSEPH ROBERDS,
> *Secretary,* W. B. WADE.

Fourth Session was held with the Pleasant Grove Church, Wabash County, August 13, 1847.
Address by Elder H. Barber.
Ministers Received: W. Hood and George Abbott.
This year $176,50 is pledged by the Church for the support of the Ministry.
At this session Elder Hood was ordained.   Elder Plummer deceased.

> *President,* J. ROBERDS,
> *Secretary,* W. B. WADE.

Fifth Annual Session was held with the Washington Township Church, August 18, 1848.

MEMBERS RECEIVED.

Elder Joseph Spencer.

CHURCHES.

Paw-Paw, Members........................50
Lagro,   " 13
Jefferson, Mich., Members...............20
Cass Co.,   "   "   5

> *President,* WM. RODMAN,
> *Secretary,* W. B. WADE.

Sixth Annual Session was held in the Jefferson Church, Michigan, August 16, 1849.

> *President,* JAMES ATCHISON,
> *Secretary,* JOHN SIMINGTON,

Seventh Annual Session was held at the Bethel Church, Elkhart County, August, 1850.

Address by Elder F. E. Thomas.

Ministers who took seats and participated: Elders T. Whitman, P. Zeigler, and F. E. Thomas; also Brothers Shiner and Barrett.

> *President,* JOSEPH ROBERDS,
> *Secretaries,* F. E. SPARLING, AND B. BENNER.

Eighth Annual Session was held with the Pleasant Grove Church, August, 1851.

Address by James Atchison.

> *President,* JOSEPH SPENCER,
> *Secretary,* JOHN SIMINGTON.

At this Session, Elders Phillip Zeigler, H. Parker, and I. B. H. Keniston were received.

Licentiates received: S. McGeorge, C. F. Wood, I. Bosley, A. Tabler, J. Gregory.

J. Gregory was ordained at this session of Conference. Deceased, Levi Abbott.

The Ninth Annual Session was held near Wolf Lake, (now Merriam Church) August, 1852.

Address by P. Zeigler.

Members Received and Ordained: Thomas Whitman. Licensed, Wm. C. Smith.

Churches: Church at Millersburg 7 members; at Osalo, Elkhart County, 15 members; Saint Joe, 13 members; Mechanicsburg, 15 members.

McGeorge ordained.

> *President,* CYRUS LOWMAN,
> *Secretary,* I. SIMINGTON,
> *Asst. Sec'y,* T. BLACK.

The Tenth Annual Session was held in Jefferson, Cass County, Michigan, August, 1853.

Address by Elder Thomas Whitman.

> *President,* J. SPENCER,
> *Secretary,* J. SIMINGTON.

The Eleventh Annual Session was held at Pleasant Grove, August, 1853.

Address by Elder Phillip Ziegler.

> *President,* T. WHITMAN,
> *Secretary,* J. SIMINGTON.

The Twelfth Annual Session was held at Waterford, August, 1854.

Address by Elder George Abbott.

Members Received: One minister and one church.

> *President,* P. ZIEGLER,
> *Secretary,* J. SIMINGTON.

The Thirteenth Annual Session was held near Wolf Lake, August, 1855.

Address by Elder Thomas Whitman.

Members Received: William B. Jones, and others united; also two churches—Millwood, 42 members; Clear Creek Huntington County, 29 members.

President, J. H. GREGORY,
Secretary, J. SIMINGTON.

The Fourteenth Annual Session was held in the Union Church, August 1857.
Members Received: For license, A. Kitlinger, and P. Winebrenner. Church at Rochester, members, 12.

President, J. H. GREGORY.
Secretary, L. GOODRICH,
Asst. Sec'y., J. CUNNINGHAM.

The Fifteenth Annual Session was held at the Clear Creek Church, Huntington County, August, 1858.
Address by P. Ziegler.
Moses McDanniel was present. Six Churches became members, and one minister, W. B. Reed.
Ordained: C. F. Wood and P. Winebrenner.

President, W. B. JONES,
Secretary, L. GOODRICH,
Asst. Sec'y., P. WINEBRENNER.

The Sixteenth Annual Session was held in the Ludlow Church, Kosciusko County, August, 1859.
Address by William B. Jones.
Ordained: H. Maddux.
Received three Churches— Rock Creek, 53 members; Warren, 22 members, and West Union, 31 members.
Licensed one—R. Freeman.

President, T. WHITMAN,
Secretary, J. CUNNINGHAM.

The Seventeenth Annual Session was held at the Pleasant Grove Church, August, 1860.
Address by Elder T. Whitman.
Ministers Received: Elders Moses McDaniel, S. C. Minnick, L. Gates, W. A. Gross, and D. E. Greer.
One Church.—Lancaster, Wells County, members, 34.

President, P. ZEIGLER.
Secretary, J. CUNNINGHAM.

The Eighteenth Annual Session was held at the Waterford Christian Church, August, 1861.
Address by Peter Winebrenner.
Several ministers united with Conference.

President, M. McDANIEL,
Secretary, J. CUNNINGHAM.

The Nineteenth Annual Session was held with the Christian Church near Wolf Lake, (now Merriam Christian Church).

Address by Abraham Snethen.

N. Summerbell was present, and lectured on Education; he spoke in the interest of Union Christian College.

One Church received.—Antioch, 40 members.

President. G. ABBOTT,
Secretary, J. CUNNINGHAM.

The Twentieth Annual Session was held in the Salimony Christian Church, Huntington County. August, 1863.

Address by N. Summerbell.

Members Licensed: David Bowser, Jacob Rittinhouse, and E. Hammon. A. Burgert was ordained.

President. P. ZIEGLER,
Secretary, J. CUNNINGHAM.

The Twenty-First Annual Session was held in the Tippecanoe Township. (Kosciusko County.) Christian Church, (Pratt's) August. 1864.

Address by Elder Thomas Whitman.

A. R. Heath was present, in the interest of Union Christian College. Jacob Rittinhouse was ordained.

President, G. ABBOTT,
Secretary, C. CLEMONS,
Asst. Sec'y, O. GARBER.

The Twenty-Second Annual Session was held in the Waterford Christian Church, August, 1865.

Address by Elder W. A. Gross.

President, ELDER P. WINEBRENNER,
Vice Prest., R. ABBOTT,
Secretary, C. CLEMONS.

The Twenty-Third Annual Session was held in the Sugar Grove Christian Church, September 26, 27 and 28, 1866.

Address by Elder James Atchison.

A. R. Heath was present, in the interest of Union Christian College.

Acting Prest., DR. P. L. WERT.
Secretary. C. CLEMONS.

The Twenty-Fourth Annual Session was held in the Murray Christian Church. August 14 to 17, 1867.

Address by Elder William B. Jones.

President. ELDER P. ZIEGLER.
Secretary, C. CLEMONS.

The Twenty-Fifth Annual Session was held in the Millwood Christian Church. August, 1868.

Address by Elder P. Zeigler.

Ministers Received: Elder J. Earnhart. Licensed: David Hida. Henry Biglo. Simon Lee. Sister M. J. May.

Churches:—Wakarusa. members. 50; Walkerton. 32 members; Wabash City, 75; Liberty Township. 50.

Elder C. Clemons withdrew from Conference.

President, THOMAS WHITMAN,
Secretary, COMODORE CLEMONS.

The Twenty-Sixth Annual Sesssion was held in the Union Christian Church, August, 1869.

Address by Elder George Abbott.

Visitors: Elders Dixon, Maple, and Manville.

Members Received: Elder D. W. Fowler. Licensed: J. J. Markley and D. N. Miller.

Churches Received: Loon Lake, Whitley County, and Spring Hill.

President, ELDER GEORGE ABBOTT,
Secretary, PETER WINEBRENNER.

The Twenty-Seventh Annual Session was held in the Merriam Christian Church, August, 1870.

Address by J. J. Markley.

Brother Simeon Lee and Elder M. W. Cook deceased.

Churches Received: Leesburg Christian Church, and Purviance Chapel.

President, J. J. MARKLEY,
Secretary, P. WINEBRENNER.

The Twenty-Eighth Annual Session was held in the Eel River Christian Church, August, 1871.

Address by Elder Thomas Whitman.

Visitors: H. Y. Rush, J. L. Dunn, William Manville, and E. W. Humphries.

Members Received: Elder D. W. Jones.

President, ELDER T. WHITMAN,
Secretary, ELDER P. WINEBRENNER,
Treasurer, J. P. KITT.

The Twenty-Ninth Annual Session was held in the Six Mile Christian Church, Wells County, August, 1872.

Address by Elder D. W. Fowler.

Several were ordained.

Churches Received: Oak Hill, Warren and Kelso.

Ministers Received: Brothers William Miles, William Pool, and C. Kimble.

President, ELDER D. W. FOWLER,
Secretary, ELDER P. WINEBRENNER,
Asst. Sec'y, D. W. JONES,
Treasurer, J. P. KITT.

The Thirtieth Annual Session was held in the Antioch Christian Church, August 14, 15 and 16, 1873.

Members Received: Elder W. S. Manville.

President, ELDER D. W. JONES,
Secretary, ELDER P. WINEBRENNER,
Treasurer, J. P. KITT.

These officers have been continued every year up to this time, except at the next Annual Session Elder D. Hidy presided.

The Thirty First Annual Session was held in the Paw Paw Christian Church, August 12 to 15, 1874.

Members Received: Ministers. Elder J. L. Dunn, E. Gleason, and C. C. Morris.

Churches: Hopewell, Rock Creek, and Beach Grove.

Conference Incorporated.

Samuel McNeely ordained.

The Thirty-Second Annual Session was held in the Christian Church near Coesse, Whitley County. August 11 to 14, 1875.

Brother William Miles deceased.

Visitors: T. C. Smith, President Union Christian College, P. Zeigler, and Moses McDaniel.

Address by Elder George Abbott.

The Thirty-Third Annual Session was held in the Pleasant Grove Church, August 16 to 19, 1876.

Address by Peter Winebrenner.

Visitors: Elders P. McCullough, A. C. Hanger, and C. W. Garoutte.

The Thirty-Fourth Annual Session was held in the Sugar Grove Christian Church, August 15 to 18, 1877.

Address by Elder Thomas Whitman.

Ministers Received: Wilson D. Samuels, M. V. Hathaway, M. K. Zorger, C. V. Strickland, and Elder J. A. Rubelt.

The Thirty-Fifth Annual Session was held in the Murray Christian Church, August 15 to 17, 1878.

Address by Peter Winebrenner.

The Thirty-Sixth Annual Session was held in the Millwood Christian Church, August 13 to 16, 1879.

Address by W. S. Manville.

Visitors: H. Y. Rush, Dayton, Ohio: W. T. Warbinton, Hagarstown, Indiana; and others.

Received the Sparta Church.

Elder A. Burgert deceased.

The Thirty-Seventh Annual Session was held in the Union Christian Church, Whitley County, August 11 to 14, 1880.

Address by Elder Thomas Whitman.

Visitors: Elder Joel Thomas, D. W. Fowler, and Sister Jennie Thompson.

> *President,* D. W. JONES,
> *Vice Prest.* C. V. STRICKLAND,
> *Secretary,* P. WINEBRENNER,
> *Asst, Sec'y,* J. P. KITT,
> *Treasurer,* J. P. KITT.

TIME AND PLACES OF HOLDING THE ANNUAL CONFERENCE:

MINISTERS AND MEMBERS.

Number of Ordained Ministers.......................... 24
    "   Unordained.............................. 7
    "   Churches................................. 31
    "   Male Members,........................1,000
    "   Female,................................1,646
Number added this year......................... 200
Aggregate Membership Reported,.................2,646

FINANCES.

Aggregate Amount of Pastor's Salary.............$ 3,400
   "   "   Paid for other Preaching........ 700
   "   "   Paid for Building Purposes..... 3,000
   "   Value of Church Property................. 34.400
   Total Amount of Money Paid out............... 7,100

SUNDAY SCHOOLS.

Number of Sunday Schools........................... 28
   "   Scholars...........................1,758
   "   Officers and Teachers.................. 317
   "   Sunday School Heralds taken............. 700
   "   Other Sunday School Papers taken.......1,100
   "   Sunday School Scholars joined Church ... 165
Aggregate of all Monies Raised by Sunday School.. $400

MISCELLANEOUS.

Number of Meeting Houses........................... 22
Ministers Enrolled at this time.................... 31
State Conference Fund, Two Years..................$15 00
Conference Incorporated............................ 1874

DELEGATES TO STATE CONFERENCE 1880.

Elder S. McNeely, Argos.
Peter Winebrenner, Merriam.
C. V. Strickland, Waterford.
W. D. Samuels, North Manchester.
Franklin Shaffer, Warren.
Elish Chrisman, Warren.

P. WINEBRENNER, *Secretary.*

LIST OF MINISTERS WITH THEIR ADDRESS.

1 Abbott, George Liberty Mills.
2 Atchison, James Pierceton.
3 Whitman, Thomas, Pierceton.
4 Rittinhouse, Jacob Wawaka.
5 Winebrenner, Peter Merriam.
6 Hidy, David North Manchester.
7 Samuels, W. D. North Manchester.
8 Strickland, C. V. Waterford Mills.
9 McNeely, S. Argos.
10 Markley, J. J. Murray.
11 Purdue, William Warren.
12 Singer, John North Manchester.
13 McGinnis, D. A. New Holland.

14 Jones, D. W. Fort Wayne.
15 Abbott, N. H. Mount Etna.
16 Manville, W. S. Valparaiso.
17 Morris, C. C. Warren.
18 Miller, V. R. Goshen.
19 Kimbal, U. Notingham.
20 Gregory, J. H. Walkertou.
21 Maddox, H. Coesse.
22 Jones, William B. Millwood.
23 Horn, J. T. Mankato, Kansas.
24 Robbinson, S. Wakarusa.
25 Stewart, G. B. Wakarusa.
26 Zorger, M. K. Laud.
27 Arnold, Martin.
28 Freeman, Riley Urbana.
29 Miller, D. N. Millwood.
30 Fanning, Jesse North Manchester.

CHURCH AND CLERK'S ADDRESS.

Church.	Clerk and Post Office.
1 Waterford	B. Benner, Waterford.
2 Millwood	J. Whiteleather, Millwood.
3 Antioch	J. C. Schroll, North Manchester.
4 Clear Creek	D. Kaylor, Huntington.
5 Pleasant Grove	D. Abbot, Liberty Mills.
6 New Madison	J. Foust, New Madison.
7 Six Mile	L. Prillman, Bluffton.
8 Sugar Grove	C. Myers, Collamer.
9 Union	Lewis Bayman, Collamer.
10 Spring Hill	J. Growcock, Ligonier.
11 Leesburg	J. A. Lay, Leesburg.
12 Merriam	J. P. Kitt, Merriam.
13 Broadway	S. Ohlwine, Ligonier.
14 Eel River	W. Messimore, Pierceton.
15 Oak Hill	J. E. Knappe, Wolf Lake.
16 Sparta	William K. Wolf, Ligonier.
17 Murray	Samuel Straw, Murray.
18 Purviance	J. M. Coulter, Mount Etna.
19 Pleasant Hill	G. W. Conrad, Wawaka.
20 Coesse	D. A. Morse, Coesse.
21 Paw Paw	R. L. Amber, Urbana.
22 Warren	F. Schaffer, Warren.
23 Wakarusa	J. W. Sellers, Wakarusa.
24 Rock Creek	J. Johnson, Barber's Mill.
25 Markle	William Keller, Markle.
26 Collamer	H. Banta, Collamer.
27 Swamp College	S. Welsh, Hartford City.
28 Kelso	Miller Morgan, Majenica.
29 Hivel's Corners	H. Simpson, Columbia City.
30 Salamonia	D. A. McGinnis, New Holland.
31 Wawaka	

SUNDAY SCHOOL SUPERINTENDENTS.

Name of School.   *Superintendent and Address.*

1 Wakarusa.................................J. W. Sellers, Wakarusa.
2 Waterford...
3 Milwood................................D. N. Miller, Milwood.
4 Antioch....................James Winesburg, North Manchester.
5 Clear Creek............................W. F. Gill, Huntington.
6 Pleasant Grove..............................D. S. Calhoun.
7 New Madison........................John Honius, New Madison.
8 Six Mile............................A. T. Studebaker, Bluffton.
9 Sugar Grove..............................H. Switzer, Collamer.
10 Union................................Alex. Bayman, Pierceton.
11 Spring Hill............................E. A. Culver, Ligonier.
12 Leesburg.............................S. B. Barker, Leesburg.
13 Merriam..............................G. W. Ott, Merriam.
14 Broadway........................William Knappe, Ligonier.
15 Eel River.......................William G. Norris, Eel River.
16 Oak Hill, 1st......................John Buchels, Wolf Lake.
   Oak Hill, 2nd..........................S. Bonner, Wolf Lake.
17 Murray.............................J. R. Harvey, Murray.
18 Purviance............................J. Purviance, River.
19 Pleasant Hill......................J. H. Swigert, Wawaka.
20 Coesse...............................D. S. Morse, Coesse.
21 Paw-Paw.............................G. E. Long, Urbana.
22 Warren.....................C. V. Strickland, Waterford Mills.
23 Rock Creek....................J. T. Mossburg, Barber's Mills.
24 Swamp College, 1st...........................E. Johnson.
   "   "   2nd...............................L. Welsh.
25 Salimony.............................D. A. McGinnis.
26 Kelso..................................Miller Morgan,

Eastern Indiana Conference.

------:0:------

ORGANIZATION AND OFFICERS.

The Eastern Indiana Christian Conference was organized near Bluffton, Indiana, September 9th, 1839.

OFFICERS.

President, ELDER DANIEL LONG.
Secretary, ELDER JAMES WILLIAMSON.

Charter Churches—Granville, Sardinia, Harrison, Walnut Creek, Jacksonville, Three-Mile, Fort Recovery, Springborough, White River, and Nettle Creek.

Total Amount of Churches.................. 10
"   "   Members..................370
Number of Ordained Ministers............. 7
"   Unordained....................... 3

PRESENT NUMBER OF MINISTERS AND MEMBERS.

Number of Ordained Ministers........... 65
"   Unordained "   15
"   Churches......................... 67
"   Added this Year 400
Aggregate Membership....................5,400

SUNDAY SCHOOLS.

Number of Sunday Schools supported.......... 23
Aggregate Number of S. S. Scholars.............. 1,935
"   "   Officers and Teachers.... 225
Number of S. S. Heralds taken........................ 1,600
"   Other S. S. Papers taken................ 800
Proportion of S. S. Scholars Joined Church........2 4-10
Aggregate of all Monies Raised by S. S.........168 90

FINANCE.

Aggregate Amount of Pastor's Salary.			..	3,671 50
"	"	Paid for other Preaching.	..	800 00
"	"	" Building Purposes, ..	..	1,252 30
..	"	Paid to Publishing House at Dayton,		500 00
Paid State Conference Fund,	..	.. ..	.. ..	5 00
" For Benevolent Purposes.	..	..	..	81 00
Aggregate Value of Church Property,			..	54,450 00
Total Amount of Monies Paid Out,				4,849 24

MISCELLANEOUS.

Number of Meeting Houses,			60
Preaching Service per Month,		..	1 3-10
Converts Baptized During the Year,	..	..	200

Conference was Incorporated in 1837.

DELEGATES TO STATE CONFERENCE.

Elders T. A. Brandon. E. Burch, D. S. Davenport. Brothers T. A. Burns. Anderson Case, R. Hayworth, and David Miller.

PRESENT OFFICERS.

President. T. ADDINGTON, *Winchester, Indiana.*
Secretary. T. A. BURNS, *Versailles. Ohio.*

In 1879 Elder John Burkitt was President.

North Western Indiana Conference.

——:o:——

This Conference was organized at Mount Pleasant, Cass County, Indiana, August 31st, 1844, and was at first called the Tippecanoe Christian Conference.

After prayer, by J. Adkins, Deacon Ira Smith was chosen to *Preside*, and Chandler Moore *Secretary*.

MINISTERS.

Ordained: Abraham Snethen, J. Adkins, Alexander Briggs, William Snethen, and William McLucas.

Licentiates: Nicholas C. Myres and Enos H. Stewart.

CHURCHES.

Salem Christian Church. Tippecanoe. Mill Creek. Big Creek. Michigantown. Rock Creek, Keen's Creek, Mount Pleasant, Indian Prairie, Kirkland, Kokomo, Honey Creek, Rattle Snake, Frankfort, Hinkle's Creek, 15. Membership, 589.

VISITORS.

Elder Joel Thomas and Leonard Shoemaker.

For fifteen years Deacon Ira Smith was continued the chief presiding officer. In 1859 John Abbott was elected his successor in the office, who was continued President of the Conference until 1869, when William Y. Winegardner was duly elected his successor, who held the office until 1871, at which time Charles G. Cox was elected President, holding his office up to the present time, 1880.

SECRETARIES:

C. C. Moore held the office of Secretary from the first up to 1858, at which time Brother Samuel Ward was duly elected his successor in office, who held the Secretarie's office up to his death, which occurred in 1875. He was an efficient and faithful servant up to the last. After his death in 1875, B. B. Lesh was duly elected, who has faithfully discharged the obligations resting upon the Secretary up to the present date, 1880.

FIRST TREASURER.

Brother Samuel Smith. M. V. Copeland was afterwards duly elected and continues to hold and perform the duties of this responsible office up to the present, 1880.

The Thirty-Sixth Annual Session of this Conference was held at Argos, Marshall County, August 6th 1879, at which time the New Constitution was adopted, and the name changed from Tippecanoe, to that of the North Western Indiana Christian Conference, by which name it is now known. Embracing the following counties, viz: Miami, Cass, Fulton, Marshal, St. Joseph, Laporte, Stark, Pulaski, White, Carroll, Tippecanoe, Benton, Jasper, Lake, Porter, and Newton.

INCORPORATION.

The Conference was Incorporated August 9th, 1880.

TRUSTEES.

J. Herring, J. R. Cox, John Himes, B. B. Lesh, William Pearson, M. V. Copeland. •

REPORTED NUMBERS AND AMOUNTS.

Ministers Reported,	21
Churches,	16
The Argos Church not Reported adds	1
	—
Total Number,	17
Total Membership Including Argos,	1,000
Number of Church Houses,	13
Value of Church Property,	$14,000

OFFICERS:

President, C. G. Cox, *New Waverly, Cass County, Indiana.*
Secretary, B. B. Lesh, *Burrows Station, Carroll County, Indiana.*
Treasurer, M. V. Copeland, *Bloomingsburg, Indiana.*

MINISTER'S NAMES AND ADDRESS.

1 Greer, J. G. Idaville.
2 Winegardner, W. Y. Greentown.
3 Snethen, Ezekial Lake City.
4 Hubartt, Thomas North Judson.
5 Shaw, Eli Lake City.
6 West, Kendall E. Logansport.
7 Rhinehart, William J. Pulaski.
8 Reed, Alexander Idaville.
9 Little, Thomas Grant.
10 Feece, William Grant.
11 Fowler, D. W. Wabash City.
12 Westfall, William H. Bringhurst.
13 Dunfee, Joseph Winamac.
14 Atwood, James Logansport.
15 Copland, Elijah Bloomingsburg.
16 Merideth, Orange.   ··
17 Webster, T. S. Hoover.
18 Critchfield, J. D. North Judson.

19 Gates, Lorison Valparaiso.
20 Thomas, John Stockton.
21 Wooley, M. N. Pulaskiville.

CHURCHES AND SECRETARIES.

Name of Church.	Secretary and Address.	Members
1 Thomas Chapel,	G. Hopkins, Carroll, members	52.
2 Twelve Mile,	T. S. Skinner, Twelvemile, "	85
3 Eel River Chapel,	T. Tyson. Hoover, "	84
4 Pipe Creek,	L. B. Lowman, Dow, "	72
5 Thomas School House,	Wm. Hiloy. Idaville, "	42
6 Tippecanoetown,	James Hill, Tippcanoet'n, "	48
7 Shiloh,	Martha Busard, Logansport, "	41
8 Grafton,	Julia E. Wood. Pulaskiville, "	24
9 Rock Creek Valley,	T. Hipshire, Logansport, "	25
10 Millark,	J. Herring, Rochester, "	62
11 Indian Creek,	Mary Young, Hirdle, "	46
12 Keep's Creek,	J. Himes, Logansport, "	44
13 Bloomingsburg,	M. V. Copeland, Bloom'sburg, "	103
14 Rock Creek,	G. W. Smith, Burrows, "	71
15 Rattlesnak,	M. Numan, Idaville, "	34
16 Crooked Creek,	L. Nethercutt, Logansport. "	85
17 Argos,	J. N. Hess, Argos, "	

No Sunday Schools are reported. How many ministers and churches have not reported we are unable to say; but as far as it goes, we have reason to believe the report is correct. Secretary, B. B. Lesh,.

Central Indiana Conference.

———— :o: ————

This Conference was organized A. D. 1824, by David Douglas, Joseph Ashley, and others. The names of the officers at the organization is marked, "Unknown."

MINISTERS AND MEMBERS.

Number of ordained ministers.................................18
Number of unordained ministers............................. 2
Number of churches belonging to Conference............. 15
    Number of members added this year, 1880, ...200.

SUNDAY SCHOOLS.

Number of Sunday Schools supported.........................9
  "   officers and teachers.......................................54
  "   Sunday School Heralds taken........................200

FINANCES.

Aggregate of pastors' salaries. $1000
  "   paid for other preaching..................................... 75
  "   paid for building purposes............................$11,400
  "   paid to Publishing House at Dayton. 2,000
  "   paid to Union Christian College........................ 500
State Conference Fund.. 10
Value of all Church property,................................$12,000

MISCELLANEOUS.

Number of Meeting Houses,......................................10
Preaching services. once per month.
Communions. once per month.
Number of converts baptized during the year. 28

DELEGATES TO STATE CONFERENCE.

Elders P. J. Baker, A. N. Downey, and J. W. Carney.

OFFICERS OF CONFERENNE.

President, J. W. CARNEY, *Taylorsville.*
Secretary, LUTE OWINGS.

Minister's Names,   *Post-Office Address.*

1 Wilson, G. R. Christiansburg, Brown co.
2 Witters, G. W. Milroy, Rush county.
3 Smith, S. Freetown, Jackson county.
4 Roberts, D. Moor's Hill, Dearborn county.
5 Comings, J. Mooney, Jackson county.
6 Anderson, Job, Milroy, Rush county,
7 Osborn, A. Mooney, Jackson county.
8 Dawson, G. Fairland, Shelby county.
9 Pavey, Samuel, Mooney. Jackson county.
10 Downey, A. S. Taylorsville, Bartholamew county.
11 Reeves, A. S. Nashville, Brown county.
12 Linley, J. Medora, Jackson county.
13 Hungate, S. Mooney, Jackson county.
14 Carmichael, H. Knightstown, Henry county.
15 Baker, P. J. Manilla, Rush county.
16 Carney, J. W. Taylorsville, Bartholamew county.
17 Hughes, Martin, Mooney, Jackson county.
18 Noble, J. Pike's Peake, Brown county.

There are twenty ministers belonging to the Central Conference, but we have eighteen names only, as above.

The number of Churches are given, but the number of members are not; hence we cannot give them.

This Report came to hand since our suming up, and is, therefore, not included therein. We have not been able to get any report at all from the Grant County Conference, but have given just as full an account of seven of the eight Conferences of Indiana, as I have been able to get. And now you have it; and may God bless it to the good of our common Christianity in the State of Indiana.

PETER WINEBRENNER.

A List of Ministers

IN THE STATE OF INDIANA, WITH POST-OFFICE ADDRESS.

————:0:————

A

Abbott, George, Liberty Mills.
Abbott, N. H. Mount Etna.
Addington, T. Winchester.
Akers, A. J. Pimento.
Akers, Thomas, Nottingham.
Allison, A. H. Millville.
Allen, T. J. Kirk's X Roads.
Achison, James, Pierceton.
Atwood, James, Cutler.
Arnold, Martin, Silver Lake.

B

Baker, P. J. Manilla.
Bannon, L. W. Russell's Mills.
Bozell, George, Shieldsville.
Brandon, T. A. Union City.
Brodrick, A. W. East Germant'n.
Brown, J. M. Staunton.
Burket, Eli, Warren.
Byrkitt, John, Knightstown.
Buman, J. T. Jamestown.
Burch, E. Blountsville.

C

Campbell, John, Newburg.
Capron, L. Harrisville.
Carney, A. L. Pleasant Hill.
Carney, J. W. Taylorsville.
Coate, W. T. Winchester.
Comer, James, Tipton.
Comer, John, Centre.
Comer, Joseph, Centre.
Coonse, J. Ridgeville.

Cummins, John, Nashville.
Cummins, J. H. Elkinsville.
Coombs, W. N. Jamestown.
Coy, Linsey Mc. Waynetown.
Compton, Squire, Brazil.
Carr, Mrs. E. Crawfordsville.
Copland, Elijah, Bloomingsburg.

D

Dawson, George, Fairland.
Davenport, D. S. Harrisville.
Dickens, J. Harveysburg.
Dipboy, J. Frankton.
Downey, A. S. Taylorsville.
Dunfee, Joseph, Winnimac.
Dykes, J. P. Middletown.
Dooley, Mrs. M. Ludlow, Ill.
Dooley, Mary, Veedersburg.

E

Ealy, Wm. M. Staunton.
Evans, D. J. Zanesville Ohio.
Ealy, Wm. Centre Point.
Evans, J. W. Crawfordsville.

F

Fanning, Jesse, N. Manchester.
Fifer, E. Straughns Station.
Fowler, D. W. Wabash City.
Feece, Wm. Grant.

G

Gillispie, T. C. Brazil.
Gates, Lorison, Valparaiso.
Gettinger, H. Merom.
Gibson, John, Muncie.

Gleason, E. S. Treaty.
Goldsberry. Isaac, Galveston.
Graves. H. Merom.
Green, A. J. Royerton.
Greer, J. G. Idaville.
Gregory. J. H. Walkerton.
Goot, R. H. Hillsborough.
Gunckle, J. M. Parker.

H

Heard, B. Fairmount.
Heath. A. R. Merom.
Hedlin, William. Rock Creek.
Heflin, F. R. Taylorsville.
Hendrix. E. M. Knightstown.
Hendrix, Wm. Knightstown.
Hidy, David, North Manchester.
Holiday. Oliver, Midville.
Hollingsworth. N. Crawfordsville
Hollingsworth. Eliza,   "
Hubartt, George, Majenica.
Hubartt, Thomas, North Judson
Hughes. M. Leesville.
Hutts. L. W. Steam Corners.
Humphrey. A. Farmland.
Harper. William. Waynetown.
Harty, D. Logansport.
Human, J. B. Jones Station.

I

Irby. Columbus. Sharpsville.

J

Johnson. L. W. Losantville.
Johnson, I. V. D. R. Bloomingsp't
Jones. William B. Millwood.
Julian. M. P. Nettle Creek.
Jones. Elza. Terre Haute.
Jacobs. Jesse, Boundry City.

K

Kimble. Uzal, Nottingham.
King, Wm. A. Neff.
Kobb, John R. Centre.

L

Ludlow, Watson, Veedersburg.
Leavell, J. W. Cadiz.
Lindsey. J. Medora.

M

McConaha. D. Idaville.
Meredith. O. Bloomingsburg.
McConnel. Hannah, Newtown.
McCoy, Robert. Medora.
McGinnis, D. A. New Holland.
McNealy. Samuel, Argos.
Maddox, Hezekiah. Coesse.
Martin, Jonathan, Mace.

Markley. J. J. Murray.
Morris, C. C. Warren.
Miller, V. R. Goshen.
Miller, D. N. Millwood.
Manville, W. S. Valparaiso.
Maple. James. Marion.
Marshall. J. H. Logansport.
Martindale, Wm. Logansport.
Miller, T. McCutcheonville.
Miller. Wm. Owensville.
Moon. R. Bennett's Switch.
Murphy, M. Newbern.

N

Noblet. John. Marble.
Nickels. J. S. Wallace.

O

Overturf. Ira. Valparaiso.

P

Phillips. J. T. Graysville.
Parr. Jesse A. Lebanon.
Pearce. Z. A. Huntsville.
Paget. J. W. Hoozierville.
Patrick. F. M. Wallace.
Parker, W. G. Summitville.
Patterson. J. J. Staunton.
Pavey, Samuel. Mooney.
Perkins, Adam. New Lancaster.
Prather, J. A. Gessie.
Priest, H. Nottingham.
Puckett. T. J. Nottingham.
Puckett, J. L. Cassville.
Perdue. William. Warren.

Q

Quick, E. Prairie Edge.
Quillen, Thomas. Mace.
Quick, Nathan, Crawfordsville.

R

Rinehart. W. J. Pulaski.
Reed. Alexander, Idaville.
Rinttihouse, Jacob, Wawaka.
Roberds, James, Eaton.
Roberds, D. Sparta.
Ross, W. D. Parker.

S

Simonds. E. D. Steam Corners.
Sowers. E. P. Harveysburg.
Smith, T. C. Merem.
Shoemaker, D. M. Cynthiana.
Sneathen, Z. Lake City.
Salee, N. Burlington.
Samuel, W. D. N. Manchester.
Seright, A. Milroy.
Shaw, Eli, Lake Scicott.

Smith, T. Mier.
Smith, Samuel, Freetown.
Smith, A. State Line City.
Smuck, Eli. Hackleman.
Spade, D. F. Portland.
Spade, William, Mills Corners.
Stewart, G. B. Wakarusa.
Stone, Conway, Rensellear.
Strickland, C. V. Waterford Mills.
Suit, John, Russiaville.

T

Tanner, E. P. Bloomington.
Teegarden, M. Bryant.
Terrell, William, Windsor.
Terrell, G. W. Windsor.
Teter, M. L. Goldsmith.
Thomas, J. Galveston.
Thompson, Jeannie, Warren.
Thompson, J. Shelbyville.
Tillman, E. Logansport.
Thomas, J. Stockton.
Trite, Thomas, Grant.
Taylor, Thomas, Crawfordsville.
Thomas, Joel, Arcanum, Ohio.

V

Van Ness, F. Tipton.

Vinson, H. Union City.
Valkenburg, S. Newtown.

W

Warbinton, W. T. Hagarstown.
Wilkins, Z. M. Veedersburg.
Webster, T. S. Hoover.
Westfall, W. H. Bringhurst.
Winegardner, W. Y. Greentown.
West, K. E. Logansport.
Whitman, Thomas, Pierceton.
White, Adelia, Spiceland.
Whit, J. C. Hackleman.
Wildman, J. D. Geneva.
Wiley, A. M. Franklin.
Williams, A. C. Mechanicsburg.
Wilson, W. Wagoner Station.
Winebrenner, Peter, Merriam.
Witters, G. W. Milroy.
Wolverton, A. Albany.
Wright, W. R. Fort Branch.
Wooley, M. N. Pulaskiville.
Wooten, H. Jordan.

Y

Yokum, B. F. Brazil.
York, B. F. Clifford.

————:o:————

The above list gives us one hundred and ninety-eight names of ministers, ordained and un-ordained, in the State, and we have reason to believe that this list is minus a number more—what the name or where they live we have no means of knowing—owing to the incomplete reports which came into our hands, and from which the list was made up, together with the Christian Almanac.

Summing Up and Remarks.

—:0:—

Total Reported Membership in the State of Indiana:

MINISTERS... 2 50
CHURCHES.. 2 00
MEMBERSHIP,..14 651
CHURCH HOUSES.......................................1 50
SUNDAY SCHOOLS,..................................... 2 00
PAID PASTORS.......................................$13 000
VALUE OF CHURCH PROPERTY........................ $134 120

For further Statistics we refer the reader to the Conferences, severally.

—:0:—

REMARKS.

The foregoing Statement presents only our reported strength, and not our *real* strength. One Conference has given us no report at all, and some of those which we have are meagre in several important particulars, and we have no means of knowing the exact number of members, finances, etc. In fact we do not understand that either of the seven Conferences reporting pretend to give their full strength,—only those reporting at their last sessions, and of these there is no small *percentage* of ministers, churches, and Sunday-schools which failed to send in their Annual Reports.

We are approximating, however, toward a correct knowledge of our whole strength, numerically and otherwise, in the State.

As we have 14.651 members reported, lacking only 349 of 15,-000, we can now be certain that our numerical strength is from fifteen to twenty thousand—probably very nearly approaching the latter figures. This may not be all that we expected; yet when we consider that this number is more than doubled by those that attend upon our ministry, and hold to the liberal views of our denomination, and in various ways add much to the interest 'and strength of the Christians, we should feel encouraged to put forth greater efforts for the spread of the Gospel of CHRIST JESUS.

Indeed, the very thought that over *forty thousand* of our fellow-creatures being reached regularly by the Christian Ministry, should fully arouse us to a sense of our duty to both God and man! Why, the fields in Indiana are white already for the sickle! Brother Reaper, (minister) thrust in thy sickle! God will help thee to gather in the golden sheaves! The field is indeed inviting. Shall we not go forward? What say you, my Brethren?

I think the field to be somewhat inviting to our State Paper. Let us see: We must have at least 6000 male members within the State, and certainly 2500 of these ought to be taking THE CHRISTIAN AGE. The lack of brethren to make up this number could be supplied by sisters who are enterprizing enough to subscribe for the paper. Then certainly quite a number—amounting to a few hundreds—could be obtained outside of Indiana; so that the out-look for our paper is hopeful. A little more earnest work in the spirit of the Master is what is needed.

DEAR BRETHREN: In getting up this Catalogue we have done the best we could under the circumstances. The time was short, as it was expected that we would have the work ready for mailing in January. We addressed quite a number of brethren, requesting such information as they might be able to give. Some have responded promptly and satisfactorily, and they have our thanks; while some did not respond at all—even some to whom I sent addressed and stamped envelops in which to return answers to our enquiries. But now you have the Catalogue, and if it meets your expectations it is well; but if not and you censure us, we must abide the decision, and rest under your censure, but must contend that we have done the best we could under the circumstances.

My Brethren, I know you will admit this fact—that this is the best Christian Catalogue of Indiana that was ever published. Accept this one now, and let us hope that next year some one will be able to give us a full and complete publication of the statistics of THE CHRISTIANS IN INDIANA.

And now a Happy New Year, and a prosperous season to you, all; and may God bless you all.

Your Brother, PETER WINEBRENNER.

PROSPECTUS
VOLUME 5,
OF

The Christian Age,

Organ of the Christian Denomination in Indiana.

WITH January 1881, THE AGE commenced its Fifth year of publication. In April, 1879, it was adopted as the organ of the Christian Denomination in Indiana for local purposes, and as a medium of intercommunication in connection with our State Mission Work.

The strength and encouragement it received by this recognition of the State Conference, and the consequent addition of patronage, has been most propitious and tended largely to make the paper a financial success.

THE AGE has also been highly commended by it readers wherever received, and is now believed to be a valuable, even indispensible auxilliary to the christian work now being prosecuted in the State and the cause generally.

IT now circulates in Illinois, Iowa and Kansas ; a few copies in the States of Ohio, Michigan, New York and New England, besides in Indiana, where the bulk of its subscribers reside,—and is slowly, though constantly increasing.

The feeling which was apparent at the commencement of its publication—that it was designed as a rival to the *Herald of Gospel Liberty*—has now about subsided, and THE AGE is being recognized as simply a *co-worker ;*—not in the same field, but in the same cause, and in *a* field peculiarly its own.

IT aims to stimulate and increase the interest in mission work and church extension, together with both a better preparation of the ministry for their work and a better support, as also a higher order of intelligence in the membership. It holds that *work* is as necessary to christian life as faith ; and that a more active zeal in the cause of the Master is the sole condition upon which our denominational existence and prosperity depends.

The editor will endeavor, from many year's experience in the profession, as well as from consciencious regard for truth and fairness, to guard the columns of THE AGE from pernicious matter, or from unchristian attacks upon the character or standing of any of its correspondents.

Address **Elder DAVID W. JONES,** *Publisher.*

Fort Wayne, Ind.